How To Help Someone With PTSD

The Ultimate Guide On How To Help Someone With Trauma

Stephanie Mike

Table of Contents

Chapter 1

Understanding PTSD

A person may develop post-catastrophic stress disorder (PTSD) if they are involved in or witness a catastrophic event that poses a substantial risk to their lives. Traumatic situations can make us feel like our lives are out of control, making it difficult to feel safe and trust other people, ourselves, and our judgments. Our experiences frequently feel unfair, unjust, brutal, and cruel, prompting us to reconsider our beliefs about the world and people. We can lose faith and withdraw from others.

It is common to have these emotions, as well as disturbing recollections, feeling on edge, or having difficulty sleeping after such an event; but, if symptoms persist for more than a few months and interfere with your daily life, you may have PTSD. A typical reaction to an unusual event is PTSD.

It is predicted that 50% of people will face trauma at some point in their lives. A traumatic experience is defined by its ability to elicit fear, helplessness, or terror in response to the prospect of damage or death, and as such, it can affect anyone. Traumatic occurrences include assaults, traffic accidents, natural catastrophes, spousal and child abuse, war, terrorist attacks, and traumatic childbirth. The majority of persons who have been exposed to traumatic situations feel some short-term distress, but their trauma eventually fades into a painful but non-destructive recollection. However, approximately 20% of those who suffer from stress acquire Post Traumatic Stress Disorder (PTSD).

PTSD often generates four types of symptoms:

- ❖ *Reliving the traumatic incident may take the form of flashbacks, nightmares, or intrusive memories.*
- ❖

* *Avoiding events that serve as reminders of the incident*
*
* *Negative alterations in thoughts and feelings.*
*
* *And feeling hypervigilant and scared of people and the environment around them.*

There is another subtype of PTSD known as Complex PTSD, or C-PTSD. This is frequently caused by repeated or sustained traumas and manifests similarly to PTSD, but with some additional symptoms.

When you know someone with PTSD, the world feels scary. They may experience disturbing recollections, feel agitated, or have difficulty sleeping. They may also try to avoid items that remind them of their trauma, including things they once enjoyed.

The hyperarousal associated with PTSD causes a disproportionate response to stimuli. For example, if snow fell from their home's roof, a 'normal' response would be to jump or startle, and perhaps look around. Someone with PTSD is likely to respond far more severely, springing out of their seat, whirling completely around, or cowering beneath a table, pulse racing and fists clenched, ready to meet an imagined attack.

Many PTSD patients have emotional numbness and difficulty communicating with others about how they feel, which can make them more nervous and angry. PTSD's sensations and symptoms can frequently become so overwhelming and uncomfortable that the patient begins to avoid anything related to the original trauma, which, as you can guess, can have an impact on day-to-day living.

Although there are many similar symptoms of PTSD, they do not appear the same in everyone. Furthermore, symptoms may fluctuate and vary with time, from childhood to late age.

PTSD is worsened by the fact that people suffering from it frequently acquire comorbid disorders such as depression, substance misuse, memory and cognition impairments, and other physical and mental health issues. The disease is also linked to impairments in a person's capacity to function in social or family settings, such as occupational insecurity, marital troubles and divorces, family strife, and parenting challenges.

Causes of PTSD

The human body is a wonderful system, but it is also complex, with several feedback loops connecting bodily components to the brain. If you significantly disrupt any of these loops, such as during a trauma, you can have an impact on the entire system.

PTSD is a mental health condition that can affect those who have gone through or seen a traumatic event. To put it simply, PTSD is a memory filing error caused by the brain suspending normal function during a traumatic situation. It generates a wide range of life-altering and invasive symptoms, so PTSD can cause significant discomfort and disruption of social and professional functioning, resulting in considerable problems in relationships and occupations. Symptoms normally appear within three months of the stressful experience, but they can occur years later.

Since the beginning of humankind, PTSD has affected people of all ages, genders, nationalities, and occupations. When someone is exposed to a profoundly unpleasant and traumatic scenario, their body and mind "suspend" regular processes and cope as best they can in order to survive.

This could involve reactions like 'frozen to the spot' or the contrary, 'flying away' from the threat. It has been identified that there are five primary reactions to trauma: fight, flight, freeze, fawn, and flop.

Their exposure to the traumatic incident can occur in one or more of the following ways:

- ❖ *They experienced the horrible occurrence.*
- ❖
- ❖ *They witnessed the horrible tragedy firsthand.*
- ❖

- ❖ *They discovered that someone close to them experienced or was threatened by the horrific occurrence.*
- ❖
- ❖ *They are constantly exposed to graphic details of traumatic occurrences, such as if they are a first responder to the scene of horrific events.*

Many systems in the body are placed on hold or adapted until the danger passes: the digestive system pauses, tongue muscles may stiffen up to prepare to flee or fight, the 'unimportant' work of creating memories is postponed, the heart rate rises, and pupils enlarge. This means that the mind does not create a recall of the traumatic experience in the 'regular' way.

Under normal/non-traumatic conditions, when information enters our memory system via sensory input such as what we can see, hear, taste, and smell, it must be converted into a form that the system can handle before it can be stored. If encoding does not occur owing to a stressful incident, the memory cannot be processed. Instead, it is stored randomly, in bits, in various locations across the brain.

Finally, when the mind remembers the trauma of 'filing', or it is prompted by a fragrance, a place, or a person, it does not perceive it as a memory. As it understands, 'the brain is in the middle of the harmful event; it is not 'outside' looking in on this event, and hence the entire system is not easily accessible to rational control. These flashbacks are really distressing. Reliving the experience as if it were occurring right now. The mind is capable of communicating real-time experiences of touch, taste, sound, vision, movement, and aroma in addition to the facts of what transpired and the emotions associated with the trauma. They may also appear as nightmares or persistent unwelcome memories.

These re-experiences and flashbacks are caused by the mind attempting to store the upsetting memories, and they can be extremely uncomfortable and terrifying because they constantly expose the person to the initial trauma. This dangerous response also causes other stress reactions in the body, such as increased blood pressure and heart rate, elevated blood sugar, and digestive issues. The body goes into hypervigilance, which heightens startle responses and increases awareness of external threats.

When confronted with a threat, their bodies and minds respond appropriately. However, their bodies are intended for this to be an immediate remedy, a short-term cure that allows the body to settle once the threat has been removed. However, with PTSD, it is almost perpetual. A lengthy, severe, or repeated trauma can physically harm the brain. The best comparison is that the amygdala can become stuck in the alert state. It prevents the body from running a healthy set of systems.

Stressful events excite their brain, and the disturbance associated with PTSD can be viewed as a type of "false alarm." This 'dysfunction' of the HPA system is thought to cause hippocampus injury, resulting in decreased memory. Simply said, PTSD causes physiological changes in the brain. The amygdala is responsible for fear reactions and conditioning. Trauma can cause hypervigilance and excessive fear responses by activating the amygdala and adjacent tissues. People with PTSD also have reduced function in the area of their brain that regulates inappropriate fear reactions.

As the mind attempts to comprehend the memory repeatedly, and the brain reactivates itself into 'danger' mode, the individual's degrees of awareness may shift. People who struggle with emotional control may have strong anxiety symptoms. This can manifest as both physical symptoms like, shortness of breath, tight muscles, heavy sweating, and a racing heart and mental symptoms such as being on edge, hypervigilance, avoiding reminders of the trauma, or feeling anxious.

The brain is designed to process memories, therefore the more the person avoids things such as mulling about the traumatic event, the less likely it is that any memory processing will occur, and the more likely it is that subsequent efforts to file a memory will occur automatically. This eventually leads to more nightmares, flashbacks, and intrusive memories, which lead to further hyper-arousal and emotional numbing, which leads to more avoidance, and so on. If treatment is not received, PTSD can persist for decades. This is how the symptom clusters reproduce themselves in a vicious cycle that can linger for years.

The injury is real. The injury is physical. It is not simply confusion, misplaced thought, or a symptom of a weak character. It is most definitely not a matter of 'Just get over it'. Because PTSD symptoms can sometimes compound and get worse over time rather than getting better, some people with PTSD are able to "manage" for an extended period of time without receiving assistance, but then the symptoms intensify and become unmanageable.

For treatment to be effective, information and memory processing must be complete. This is why therapies like EMDR, which help people process and work through traumatic experiences, are highly effective. Some people can completely recover from PTSD with treatment. Others may find that it reduces the severity of their symptoms. Treatment also provides patients with the tools they need to manage their symptoms so that they do not interfere with their daily lives.

Recognize PTSD in a Loved One

People suffering from PTSD struggle to make sense of what they have experienced or witnessed. They may retain disturbing visions or memories of the most unpleasant aspects of the trauma while spending a lot of time avoiding anything that would remind them of what happened. The events seem too enormous to consider or discuss. People with PTSD may retreat and spend more time by themselves because they perceive social interaction as more work and stress. Sleep and focus issues are typical since the body is so "on edge" and behaving as if the trauma is still occurring in the present time.

We also know that persons with PTSD tend to see themselves, the future, and other people in their lives through particular "mental filters. One example is that persons with PTSD frequently blame themselves for events that occurred during the trauma, which makes no sense. Some of our healthcare personnel suffer from "moral harm," blaming themselves for what they did or did not do during the worst of the pandemic.

PTSD patients may also have physical symptoms such as elevated blood pressure and heart rate, exhaustion, muscular tension, nausea, joint pain, headaches, back pain, and other types of pain. The individual in pain may not be aware of the link between their agony and a traumatic experience. For patients with persistent pain, the discomfort may act as a reminder of the traumatic incident, exacerbating PTSD symptoms. Some persons who acquire PTSD and chronic pain also suffer from depression, alcoholism, and prescription medication abuse.

The good news is that there are effective therapies for both PTSD and C-PTSD. Unfortunately, many people are unaware of their illness and do not seek therapy owing to stigma, a lack of belief in their ability to be healed, a fear of expressing their trauma, or a refusal to admit their coping difficulties.

Getting healthier means something different to each person. Many people find that treatments like EMDR and CBT completely alleviate their problems. Others experience fewer or milder symptoms. Your symptoms do not have to interfere with your daily routine, employment, or relationships.

Chapter 2

The Value of Empathy and Patience

Empathy, sympathy, and tolerance are required when caring for someone suffering from post-traumatic stress disorder (PTSD). PTSD can have a tremendous influence on a person's life, creating disturbing symptoms and influencing their relationships, career, and overall well-being. Here are some ways to help someone with PTSD lessen reactivity and hypervigilance, as well as additional symptom reduction suggestions:

Create a comfortable and nonjudgmental environment: People with PTSD frequently suffer increased anxiety and may feel constantly on edge. Make them feel safe around you by providing an environment in which they may freely express their thoughts and emotions without fear of being judged or criticized.

Be a good listener
When caring for someone suffering from PTSD, active listening is essential. Allow the individual to express their experiences, thoughts, and feelings at their own speed. Active listening involves giving them your complete attention, keeping eye contact, and affirming their feelings. Avoid interrupting or giving unsolicited advice unless they clearly request it.

Provide practical assistance
PTSD symptoms can make it difficult for people to complete ordinary duties. If they are willing, provide practical assistance such as helping with domestic tasks, doing errands, or accompanying them to appointments. These acts of compassion can help them feel less stressed and more cared for.

Encourage professional help
While you may offer support, it is important to remember that PTSD frequently necessitates expert therapy. Encourage the individual to

seek therapy or a trauma specialist in mental health who has experience treating PTSD, as well as a psychiatrist, group, and other services in your neighborhood. Offer to help them find resources or accompany them to appointments if they like.

Respect their bounds

Individuals with PTSD may have distinct triggers (physiological autonomic responses) or events that are overpowering. Respect their boundaries and do not force them to talk or confront anything that makes them uncomfortable. Let them know you're there to encourage them, but also give them space when necessary.

Show patience and understanding

Recovery from PTSD is a gradual process that may include setbacks. It is critical to be patient and empathetic, as the individual may have both good and terrible days. Validate their progress and urge them to practice self-care and kindness.

Take care of yourself

Supporting someone with PTSD can be emotionally difficult. Remember to take care of yourself and seek help from friends, family, or professionals as needed. Self-care and preserving your mental health can allow you to better serve others.

It is vital to remember that everyone's PTSD experience is unique, especially since each person's trauma experience and state of mind, as well as development, epigenetics, and other variables, all play a role in the development of PTSD. As a result, tailor your support to the individual's requirements by asking, clarifying, and observing nonverbal and verbal congruence. Discuss and challenge behaviors, not individuals. Traumatized people may internalize and suffer from survivor's guilt, humiliation, compounding losses, violations, and cumulative moral harm that has a profound impact on their sense of self or "core."

Remember that everyone's experience with PTSD is unique, so tailor your approach to the individual's requirements and preferences. By providing support, empathy, and patience, you can help someone with PTSD on their path to healing and recovery. Post-traumatic stress disorder can appear in a variety of ways that differ from ordinary anger, rage, impatience, irritability, terror, hypervigilance, and difficulty relaxing or sleeping.

Be mindful of triggers, by learning to recognize the person's trigger reactions and nonverbal cues, and knowing and being curious about what might have caused or created a visceral reaction to the fight, flight, and freeze portion of the brain linked to hypervigilance, as well as normalize and calm their amygdala, scan and internalize external and internal cues from the five senses, read other people's expressions, feelings, thoughts, and beliefs.

Assist them in managing or avoiding those situations wherever possible. If a trigger cannot be avoided, work together to create a plan for safely navigating it and providing support both during and after. Encourage healthy coping mechanisms by assisting the individual in developing and implementing healthy coping strategies such as deep breathing exercises, mindfulness techniques, physical activity, creative outlets, or engaging in activities that they love and relax in.

It's crucial to highlight that, while some symptoms may overlap with anger, annoyance, fear, or hypervigilance in other contexts, the key distinction in PTSD is their persistence, severity, and link to the traumatic incident. PTSD symptoms generally persist for more than a month and profoundly impair a person's everyday functioning and well-being.

Here are a few instances of PTSD behaviors that may be misinterpreted:

Trigger avoidance
People suffering from PTSD may go to tremendous measures to avoid people, places, activities, or situations that bring back memories of the traumatic incident. This avoidance can be misinterpreted as social retreat, introversion, or apathy, rather than a coping method for avoiding upsetting memories or triggers.

Emotional numbness

People suffering from PTSD may have a limited range of emotions and appear disconnected or emotionally distant. Instead of viewing this emotional numbing as a protective reaction to intense trauma-related feelings, it could be mistaken for apathy, a lack of empathy, or even personality traits like coldness or indifference.

Hypervigilance and startling responses

Individuals with PTSD may be quickly startled, hyper-aware of their surroundings, and overly cautious for potential hazards. These behaviors can be misinterpreted as normal worry or an overly cautious disposition, rather than being identified as signs of PTSD caused by a heightened sense of risk and an altered perception of safety.

Irritability and angry outbursts

PTSD can cause increased irritation, hostility, and even wrath. These emotional outbursts may be misinterpreted as mood swings, anger control issues, or a general poor temper, rather than as signs of a traumatic stress response.

Self-destructive Behaviors

Some people with PTSD engage in self-destructive activities, such as substance misuse, self-harm, or dangerous behavior. These acts may be misinterpreted as poor impulse control, addiction, or attention-seeking behavior, rather than attempts to cope with uncomfortable feelings or regain control.

Dissociation and Detachment

People with PTSD may suffer dissociation, a sense of being disconnected from their own body or surroundings, or memory gaps relating to the incident. These experiences may be misconstrued as absent-mindedness, memory issues, or even evidence of dissociative illness, rather than being identified as symptoms of PTSD.

Changes in beliefs and perspectives

PTSD can cause major modifications in an individual's views, values, and worldview. They may have feelings of guilt, humiliation, or a sensation that the trauma has profoundly altered their identity. These alterations can be misdiagnosed as personality changes, a crisis of identity, or even despair, rather than being recognized as the result of traumatic experiences.

It is critical to handle these behaviors with compassion and empathy, bearing in mind that they may be based in traumatic events. If you suspect someone is suffering from PTSD or another mental health problem, encourage them to get professional care from a skilled mental health practitioner to ensure an accurate diagnosis and appropriate support.

Chapter 3

Professional Treatment Alternatives

After starting treatment, some PTSD sufferers get better in six months, while others deal with the symptoms for the rest of their lives. Everyone reacts differently to traumatic experiences. Gender, previous trauma history, and other risk and resiliency factors all contribute to the progression of illness.

Nowadays, a lot of doctors believe that psychotherapy is the "gold standard" initial treatment for PTSD. In many cases, PTSD treatment includes medication, which is typically used in conjunction with psychotherapy. More people are starting to recognize alternative therapies like yoga, meditation, and acupuncture as PTSD treatments.

How to Help Treat PTSD with Oral Medication

Trauma psychotherapies are typically first-line treatments. Following a thorough mental evaluation, the treating physician may offer medication for comorbid conditions such as attention deficit hyperactivity disorder (ADHD) or depressive disorders.

Older individuals may have less effectiveness with medication-based PTSD treatment than younger patients because they do not digest medicines in the same way.

Common medications used to treat PTSD include:

Antidepressants medications help to reduce depression and anxiety symptoms. Antidepressants such as paroxetine, sertraline, and venlafaxine, which are serotonin and norepinephrine reuptake inhibitors (SNRIs) rather than selective serotonin reuptake inhibitors (SSRIs), are commonly prescribed for PTSD; however, The Food and Drug Administration (FDA) has only approved sertraline and paroxetine thus far. Side effects of these medications may include headache, nausea, muscle spasms, agitation, or issues with sexuality.

Antidepressants are also accompanied by a warning that they may increase the risk of suicide ideation in children, adolescents, and young adults.

Benzodiazepines can help you feel less anxious and stressed. Because of the possibility of abuse, they are rarely used for an extended period. Prazosin is sometimes administered to treat recurring nightmares or other sleeplessness symptoms. Prazosin side effects include fatigue, lethargy, headaches, and nausea.

How Talk Therapy Can Help Treat PTSD

Psychotherapy, sometimes known as "talk therapy," is a typical treatment in which you discuss your situation with a doctor or another mental health specialist. This sort of therapy can be done one-on-one or in a group environment.

PTSD is one illness for which evidence-based psychotherapy approaches have proven to be considerably more beneficial than medication. These methods include therapies such as prolonged exposure therapy, cognitive processing therapy, and eye movement desensitization.

A key component of the most effective therapy is talking to someone who can teach you how to manage your symptoms on your own. Essentially, the premise behind talk therapy is that it can activate a patient's flight or fight response and then assist him or her in moving thoughts from survival mode to intellectual processing sections of the brain, such as the frontal cortex. This approach, in turn, helps the patient analyze his or her experience logically and reframe the painful event so they stop blaming themselves and refrain from saying things like "if only" or "I should have."

They may receive only one type of talk therapy, or their doctor may employ a combination treatment strategy. A carefully selected and sequential therapeutic method may be necessary, depending on the traumatic experience, biopsychosocial challenges, symptom presentation, and patient preferences. Because PTSD can manifest in a variety of ways, physicians must make sophisticated judgments about how to treat it, which includes addressing a variety of ongoing stresses to assist patients manage their condition.

The phrase "talk therapy" can be deceptive because all effective PTSD therapies have a behavioral component.

Types of Talk Therapy

Prolonged Exposure Therapy
This sort of treatment allows them to face their trauma in a safe setting. It allows people to talk about the specifics of the trauma and tackle safe settings that they may have avoided. Writing or visiting the scene of the event can help individuals confront and handle their anxiety.

What helps is essentially modifying their physical and emotional responses when reminded of the experience. They may even utilize a virtual reality gadget to virtually re-enter the trauma scene.

Previous research has demonstrated the efficacy of prolonged exposure therapy: A review concluded that prolonged exposure therapy is a successful first-line therapy for PTSD, irrespective of the type of trauma.

Cognitive Process Therapy
This treatment helps you address harmful beliefs about the trauma. It may help individuals gain a fresh understanding of the traumatic

incident, resulting in fewer persistent unpleasant thoughts and symptoms.

For example, if a patient has an incorrect belief, such as "Nobody respects the rules, hence the world is not safe," this sort of treatment will assist that patient in finding alternate explanations for that data and recognizing their own biases of perception.

Stress Inoculation Training
This treatment teaches how to lessen anxiety by examining memories in a healthy manner.

Eye movement desensitization and reprocessing (EMDR).
This technique includes exposure therapy and a set of directed eye movements. The idea is to help people digest traumatic memories and adjust their responses to them.

According to one study, cognitive restructuring has a "substantial impact" and can help minimize PTSD symptoms.

Child-Parent Psychotherapy (CPP)
This is a type of psychotherapy for children up to the age of five who have been through traumatic situations or are exhibiting trauma symptoms, difficulty bonding, or behavioral issues. Promoting and enhancing the caregiver-child relationship is one of the main objectives in order to safeguard the child's development and trauma healing.

Strengthening Families Coping Resources (SFCR) is a trauma-focused, multifamily skill-building intervention that provides trauma treatment and therapeutic techniques to assist families in managing ongoing stress and potential re-exposure.

Chapter 4

Self-Care for Supporters

Caring for an individual with Post Traumatic Stress Disorder (PTSD) can be challenging and frustrating. Your own mental health may go further down your priority list, yet it is critical to look after yourself in order to provide care and support.

Many carers do not perceive themselves to be "carers" because there is no clear distinction between being a caregiver and being a supportive partner, family member, or friend.

Carers' definitions range among organizations, which can be confusing. For example, the UK welfare system has its own set of criteria for determining who is a carer and hence eligible for a Carer's Allowance. This may differ from the criteria used by your local authority to determine whether you are eligible for additional support.

Mind and other humanitarian groups have a broader understanding of what it means to be a caregiver. Caring for someone means providing practical and/or emotional support to help them deal with daily life. This description includes a variety of responsibilities, such as meal preparation, medication management, and appointment attendance, which is common among loved ones of people with PTSD.

Caring for someone with PTSD can be quite stressful. Witnessing their symptoms is frequently distressing, and listening to how they feel, while beneficial, can be upsetting. You may struggle to cope, resulting in symptoms of anxiety and despair. You may ignore your physical health, such as not getting enough sleep or exercise, which can have an impact on your mood and capacity to cope with stress. Caring for others can make you feel alone and alienated.

Self-care is also crucial because of the risk of secondary traumatization. This means that spouses, partners, and family members of those with PTSD may acquire their own symptoms. This might occur after listening to trauma stories or being exposed to frightening symptoms like flashbacks. The more drained and overwhelmed you feel, the greater the likelihood that you may get traumatized.

When you are concerned about your health, you must see your general practitioner. You do not need to be diagnosed with a mental condition to receive help. GPs are aware of the challenges that arise when caring for someone, so they may lead you to the right resources.

Counseling may be extremely beneficial for carers since it allows them to express their emotions without being judged. Some counseling is offered through the NHS, however services and accessibility vary depending on where you reside. If NHS therapy is available, your GP can refer you to it, or to a private counselor.

Citizens Advice in the various regions has information about local services that can help. They also provide many valuable internet resources.

It is critical to allow oneself some downtime on a regular basis. Spending time away from the person you are caring for might be challenging, both practically and emotionally, but it makes a significant difference.

Maintaining your physical health can have a significant impact on your overall well-being. Make an effort to eat well, exercise frequently, and get adequate sleep. Neglecting these essential self-care duties makes it more difficult to cope with the demands of caring for someone else. Planning your activities and sticking to a routine benefits both you and the person you care about. Use a planner or calendar to arrange activities, appointments, and tasks. Create a weekly to-do list, highlighting the most critical chores as priorities. Staying organized allows you to feel more in control and decreases stress.

If you feel helpless, connecting with other caregivers can be the best thing you can do. They can provide advice and coping skills. Being in contact with folks in similar situations will help you feel less isolated. Citizens Advice and your GP can connect you with local caregivers' groups, but you can also look into internet resources.

Chapter 5

Communication Strategies

Many people deal with communication issues. Communication can be more challenging when PTSD is present. Just as trauma survivors are often frightened to talk about what occurred to them, family members are sometimes afraid to confront how their loved one's PTSD affects their lives. Family members may desire to avoid discussing the difficulties. They may believe that if they don't talk about them, they will go away. Not communicating may lead to additional problems.

Creating a Comfortable Space to Talk
A calm, distraction-free environment can go a long way toward making them feel relaxed and secure. Respecting their boundaries is also important. Do not press them to discuss their trauma as they'll open up when they feel safe.

Furthermore, avoid sounding furious or aggressive. Instead, concentrate on active listening. Pay attentive attention to what they're saying and acknowledge that their feelings are real. Do not interrupt or try to correct anything.

Active Listening
Remove any distractions and truly concentrate on their speech. Maintain eye contact and occasionally nod to signal that you are interested. Acknowledge their emotions. Merely expressing your comprehension with remarks like "That sounds overwhelming" or "That must have been extremely difficult" is helpful. Avoid minimizing their experience or making disrespectful comments.

PTSD can generate a variety of reactions. Avoid any criticism or judgment. Instead, consider their perspective. Ask clarifying questions to better comprehend their experience without saying they are incorrect or exaggerating.

Open Communication

Avoid making ambiguous statements or beating about the bush. Speak honestly and directly about your intended message. Use plain language and avoid any jokes or sarcasm that could be misinterpreted.

Let them know you support and care about them, using "I'm here for you" and "You're not alone in this" are two expressions that can be quite helpful.

Start with casual topics

Before getting into difficult areas, start with frivolous conversations or similar interests to establish comfort and familiarity.

Do not press them to discuss their trauma. Sometimes kids just want to talk about their day. If you want to talk about something possibly triggering, get permission first. Give them authority over the conversation and respect their boundaries.

Responding to Triggers

Their emotions may rise in response to a stimulus. Remain calm and reassuring. Use a calming tone and let them know you're here for them. Gently tell them that they are safe in the present time. "You're secure here" or "This is a flashback, not reality" can be reassuring.

Managing Anger outbursts in PTSD

Safety First

If a person with PTSD poses an imminent threat, contact emergency services. Do not hesitate.

De-escalate with empathy

Forget yelling. Speak gently, recognize them, and establish a safe environment (silent room, remove yourself if necessary). According

to research from the Anxiety and Disorders Association of America
(ADAA), people suffering from anxiety, which frequently coexists with
PTSD, respond better to calm and compassionate speech.

Identify triggers

Loud noises, scents, crowds, and seemingly innocuous situations
can all trigger PTSD episodes. Identify probable triggers to prevent
similar circumstances, or devise a soothing strategy.

Focus on Calming Techniques

The National Center for PTSD suggests a variety of approaches for
controlling PTSD symptoms, including angry outbursts. Encourage
them to employ recognized coping methods such as deep breathing,
muscle relaxation, and mindfulness activities. If they don't have any,
suggest easy alternatives like breathing exercises or splashing cool
water on their faces.

Patience is key

De-escalation requires time. Be patient and avoid passing judgment.
Their rage derives from trauma, not you.

The solution rests in providing a safe environment through active
listening, transparent interaction, and respect for their boundaries.
Following the guidelines given above will help you create trust, foster
a deeper relationship, and be a source of strength for them on their
healing journey.

Chapter 6

Helping During a PTSD Episode

A PTSD episode can be exceedingly distressing, leaving the person feeling out of control, detached and lonely, or fearing for their life. This can be an extremely daunting experience. If you have a close relationship with someone who has PTSD, you should understand how to help them during an episode.

A PTSD episode, additionally referred to as a PTSD attack, is a period of severe symptoms that lasts many hours. The symptoms can be so severe that they impair the person's ability to work or function in everyday life. During a PTSD episode, the individual may experience intrusive thoughts, flashbacks, visions, and nightmares that remind them of the incident that produced their PTSD.

They may also experience overwhelming anxiety and fear. Physical symptoms of a PTSD episode may include shaking, sweating, racing heartbeat, and difficulty breathing. In some cases, the individual may feel as if they are losing control or about to die.

There are some things you can do to help someone calm down during a PTSD attack, which are described below:

Create a safe space.
The first step should be to create a safe environment for the individual. This entails removing any possible triggers from the environment, such as bright light and loud noises. If possible, find a quiet place for the individual to sit or lie down.

Remain calm and reassuring. Reassuring the person with positive words can make them feel more relaxed and in control. Avoiding sudden movements will also help to alleviate the individual's anxiety. It's best to speak in short, simple sentences so the listener can concentrate on what you're saying.

Encourage them to breathe slowly and evenly
Hyperventilation is one of the symptoms of a PTSD episode, and it can make the person feel even more panicked or out of control. Encourage the person to breathe slowly and evenly to help reduce anxiety and prevent future panic attacks.

Encourage them to stay in the present
People with PTSD frequently dissociate from reality during traumatic events. This means they may feel detached from their bodies or as if they are reliving a traumatic event. It is critical to encourage the individual to focus on the present moment and ground themselves in their surroundings. You can accomplish this by having them describe what they hear, feel, and see in the present moment.

Offer emotional support
It is critical that you offer emotional support and reassurance during a PTSD episode. Remind the person that they are not alone and that you are here to support them. While you listen, don't pass judgment and give supportive remarks. Helping the individual feel understood and validated can be extremely beneficial in managing their symptoms.

Encourage them to get professional help
PTSD is a progressive disorder, which means it will worsen over time if not treated. Encourage the individual to seek professional help so that they can receive the necessary treatment. This will help to prevent further PTSD attacks.

Let your loved one know that they are not alone and that you will be there for them during this difficult time can be extremely beneficial. Do not forget to encourage them to seek help from a mental health professional.

Conclusion

It can be upsetting to see an individual you care about suffer from post-traumatic stress disorder (PTSD). Here are some things you can do to help them.

PTSD can be debilitating, and the symptoms can be difficult to cope with. This is not only true for the person with PTSD; it can also be extremely stressful for loved ones, friends, and family. The condition can have a significant impact on relationships and daily activities. However, it's important to remember that, while you may feel helpless, there are several things you can do to help your loved one.

Here, we look at how you can help someone with PTSD and offer advice on how you and your loved one can manage their condition on a daily basis. We also look at how you can care for yourself while supporting a loved one with PTSD.

Learn everything about PTSD
One of the most beneficial things you can do is learn as much as possible about PTSD. This includes PTSD symptoms and how treatment works. By learning as much as possible about this mental health condition, you can gain a better understanding of why your loved one behaves the way they do and what emotions they are experiencing. This will allow you to better support them.

It's also helpful to try to pinpoint your loved one's specific triggers and warning signs. Triggers are typically specific situations that are similar to the circumstances surrounding the trauma. For instance, their PTSD symptoms could be triggered by:

- *Certain smells*
- *Loud noises.*
- *Crowds*
- *People argue.*

- ❖
- ❖ *Flashing lights.*
- ❖
- ❖ *Significant dates or seasons.*
- ❖
- ❖ *Being in situations where they feel confined or 'trapped'*

There may also be indications that they are struggling or experiencing symptoms such as flashbacks. Warning signs might include:

- ❖ *Their mood has changed*
- ❖
- ❖ *They may become anxious, angry, upset, or irritated. They may also show signs of depression or have thoughts about harming themselves.*
- ❖
- ❖ *A change in their energy levels*
- ❖
- ❖ *They may become easily distracted or hyper-alert all at once.*
- ❖
- ❖ *A change in their job performance.*
- ❖
- ❖ *They may miss deadlines or produce work that does not meet their usual standards.*

By learning their specific triggers and warning signs, you'll be able to recognize when they're struggling and anticipate situations that may be challenging for them. This will allow you to assist them when they need it the most.

Keep communicating
When dealing with someone suffering from PTSD, it is critical to maintain open lines of communication. Make sure to regularly check in with them to find out how they're doing. However, do not press them to speak if they do not wish to. Simply checking in with them demonstrates that you are always there for them and that they do not have to suffer in silence.

If they want to talk to you about what they're going through, listen to what they say. Even if they want to talk about the same things over and over, it's critical that you remain open and understanding, because this could be extremely beneficial to them and their recovery.

Avoid passing judgment
If you've never had PTSD, it can be tough to understand or empathize with your loved one's experience. However, it is critical that you reply to them in a nonjudgmental manner.

Don't ask why they didn't act differently at the time of the horrific experience, or recommend that they simply attempt to forget about it. Trauma and PTSD are unique to each individual, so it's critical to remain open-minded and help them in the way they need it, without judgment.

Be patient
PTSD is a difficult disorder, and healing takes time. That is why it is critical to be patient with your loved one and avoid putting pressure on them to recover quickly. Even if the recovery process is slow and they keep going through the same things, be with them and support them.

Assist them in finding expert support
While the ideas above might help people manage their symptoms on a daily basis, PTSD frequently requires expert care. Your loved one's primary care physician may be the first point of contact. You could encourage them to schedule an appointment and offer to accompany them as moral support. Their doctor will be able to assess their medical history and symptoms and offer appropriate treatment.

Private clinics, such as Priory, provide thorough, evidence-based PTSD treatment. This will be adjusted for each individual and is likely to comprise a combination of:

❖ *Talk therapies, like cognitive behavioral therapy (CBT)*
❖
❖ *Specialized treatment procedures, such as eye movement desensitization and reprocessing (EMDR).*
❖

Look after yourself
Supporting someone with PTSD can be difficult and exhausting. That is why it is so vital to take care of oneself.

Try to set aside time each day to do something you enjoy or find calming. This could be taking a hot bath, reading a book, or listening to music. Exercise has numerous mental health benefits, and you should also strive to eat healthily and get plenty of sleep. You can't pour from an empty cup, so looking after yourself will put you in a better position to care for your loved one.

It's also crucial to acknowledge that you may have conflicting feelings toward your loved one at times. You may be frustrated and bitter, and all you want is some 'normality'. You might then start to feel guilty as a result. However, don't beat yourself up about it. These feelings are completely normal and do not indicate that you are a horrible person.

Things to say to someone who has PTSD
There are several things you may say to someone with PTSD to help them cope with their feelings and feel better. You can:

❖   *Regularly reassure them that you will always be there to support them.*

❖

❖   *Discuss the future and develop exciting plans.*

❖

❖   *Tell them that you are confident in their ability to heal and that you will support them every step of the way.*

❖

❖   *Reinforce to them that they are safe and secure.*

❖

❖   *Highlight their skills, characteristics, and triumphs.*

❖

❖   *Validate their emotions; what they're feeling is very genuine to them. Do not dismiss or make assumptions.*

In addition to the suggestions above, there are other practical things you can do in your daily life to aid your loved one with their PTSD.

Plan for a crisis
It can be beneficial to discuss with your loved one what actions you can take together in the event of a catastrophe. Sit down with them while they are feeling quite well and discuss how you can assist them if they are ever in crisis. This may include items like:

Make a list of specialists and support agencies to call on when your loved one is struggling. These could include their GP, helplines like Samaritans, or your local Mind organization.

Encourage them to create a self-care box, which is when they fill a box with stuff that will help to divert and comfort them if they're ever in trouble.

Create a list of symptoms to watch for and triggers to be aware of.

Make a list of all medications they may be taking, including the dosage.

Ask them what they need from you
It is critical to establish with your loved one exactly what they require from you on a daily basis in order to make them feel comfortable. For example:

Would they like to have their own space, or would they like regular intimacy, such as hugs and holding hands?

Would they like it if you kept in touch with them whenever you went out, letting them know where you were and when you'd return home?

Do they want predictable routines in their daily life? If so, how do they want you to fit into their routine?